24

by

J. Whitebird

Second Coming Press

ISBN: 0-915016-21-4
Library of Congress Catalog Card No.: 78-1142

SECOND COMING PRESS
P.O. Box 31249
San Francisco, CA 94131

Other books by J. Whitebird:

The Family Hand Anthology and Collected Letters
Alpha Publishing Company

Bootstrap Chronicles
Contemporary Arts Museum of Houston

Naked
Thorp Springs Press

Spare Poems
Texas Portfolio Press

Birthmark
Second Coming Press

Editor, ***Travois, An Anthology of Texas Poetry***
Contemporary Arts Museum and Thorp Springs Press

ACKNOWLEDGEMENTS

Some of the poems in this book have previously been published in the following publications:

19 + 1: An Anthology of San Francisco Poetry (Second Coming Press)
Texas Observer
TAWTE
Voices International
Texas Portfolio
Community of Friends
Travois, An Anthology of Texas Poetry
Texas Prize Short Stories and Poems
Pawn Review
Texas Slough
Birthmark (Second Coming Chapbook)
Breakthrough Women's Newspaper

Cover by Edsel M. Cramer

Born in Houston, Edsel Maurice Cramer studied at the Chicago Art Institute, the Art Student's League in New York, and the Art League in San Francisco. After a rewarding trip to Europe, Mr. Cramer returned to the states to complete portrait assignments on the East and West coasts and in Houston where he now resides.

"I like to think of myself in some tragic way—must be all that sitting in the back of the bus."

24

by

J. Whitebird

DECISION

"each movement deliberate
as in grief,
this pain numbs the hands . . .
the wrists . . ."

whatever else we were
we were always fools
it showed in our eyes
we gave ourselves away
at the first glance

to say I'd stake my reputation on it
is to say
what kind of reputation I have

sometimes I wish
I were a virgin again
so I'd have something
to lose

on this beach
the civilized die first,
the naked lose their skins
to grow new scaley ones

bereft
between god and man
there are still such things
as morals,
the jaded live
among the web-footed intelligence
in the rocks
while I choose the open horizon
the human will

and above us all,
a fantasy of bodies merging,
the elements still hold the field

First Skin

between the poems
of cold steel
the razor words that slice,
and the winged verse
that flies
haunting with the distant cry
of homeless birds,
my words walk
fingering the soul's severed flute,
seeking to place
a small familiar sound
on the slashed landscapes
of the heart
where the birds once sang

when my mother and I
lived in the old boarding house
at Number One Dennis Street
(which we later improvised
as Baltic Avenue)
it was run by a crazy gray haired lady
with 27 cats
and her mumbling senile brother
        who lived in the room
                off the turn in the stairs
                        and made frightening noises
                                at the children as they passed

        being five
        and superstitious
        I always ran the last steps
        up to the one room we had
        by the bathroom

I remember the day
the house across the street burned down
my brothers got a bunch
of smudgy autographs from the firemen
they kept for years,
and how softly I stepped
the weekend the husband of
the-lady-down-the-hall-
with-the-six-kids
got a pass out of prison
to see them,
and how I always liked
the nine block walk
to first grade
because it was quiet
mostly, I remember
when I had rheumatic fever
my mother brought home

the brand new portable television,
how awed I was
by such a huge acquisition

Now I want Hawaii in yachts
Europe and limousines
see what the world has done to me, Mumsey?
I should have stuck
with boarding houses
and monopoly games

NORTH BEACH

My face is striped
with the door
that slammed against my drunkenness
while following you
from beer to beer
my shoulders bruised
from your hungry teeth

but,
not being between 2 a.m.
and work the next morning,
the words
"I want to see you."
are meaningless

DARK MOON
BITTER FRUIT

I ate a green apple
this morning,
thinking of you

the round, tight flesh
so tart
it puckered the lips

but the stinging memory
of last night
is worse

bitter fruit,
firm to the touch
and pleasing to the eye,
is like the tide of a dark moon

nocturnal swimmer
beware,
innocent waves
so deceiving,
lest the undercurrent
carry you away

with words
my mind is filled
but not enough
to bridge the distance
between us

I want to write
shout
sing
express
roll the sounds
off my tongue
like small acrobats
leap-blossoming from my mouth

touched off by your laughter
word mines explode in my face
half built bridges collapse
shades of sounds
overcome me,
only your face remains
suspended across a reeling sky
smiling your impenetrable Cheshire,
my acrobats offer nothing
uphold no structure
trapezes swinging wildly

too late,
I am exposed, betrayed
profaned in expression
the kiss I sought
to relive
shudders and turns cold

like
not drinking too much water
after running
or knowing when
to put down the bottle
on the first
good saturday night in months

like that
I read your letter, once
                    twice
then hide it from myself
in the drawer marked
miscellaneous
so as not to come away
too bloated on your words

in six months
I will clean out the drawer
throw most of it away
and file the rest
to be thrown away later

then
I will carefully
unfold the letter
pretending to myself
I have forgotten its contents
and am merely
rereading it out of curiosity
not greed
or
        desperation

YOU
THE INSPIRATION

finger-singing
conjurer,
play me a tune
laugh-dancing
I following after
fearful
tear-stepping

wind piper
either lead me
inside the still mountain
to lie down
in the Beautiful Cage
or take your music
out of my ears
and leave me alone
with my mockingbirds

HE WAS
A DISCIPLINE
I PERFORMED ON MYSELF
LIKE A DELICATE SURGERY

snake dancing
coaxing the cobra
I begged redemption
from the fangs

he coiled
like a candle flame
like smoke
all illusion
but the bite

now
when I dance,
no longer stunned
by beauty,
accustomed to the terror
of imagined perfection,
I seek the strongest partner
dare the worst poisons

I tease destruction
to win again
the sacred inspiration

flinging my love
against the world
like a weapon
I feel the backlash
of my own defenses

and somewhere within
a dark child cries

SHADOWS

we are known
by no one
but ourselves

this vague
passionate
hierarchy
breeds secrets
hidden motives
in back alleys of our lives

we will never
break out of the paths
we were given
and we shall always
pretend we have

for lack
of a better form
we are human

for lack
of a better word
we call ourselves poets

for lack of knowledge
to handle
the love inside
we turn the claws
of remorse
against each other
harpies of guilt
tear out our eyes

birth frightens us
death relieves us
the distance between
we fill
with worlds of words

our poems
have no end
the lines lead
in and out
of shadows

we learn
to crave the claws
long for the shadows
to overtake us

the masks we wear
are stone fortresses
destruction is the only thing
we are capable
of acknowledging

WHILE READING JEAN GENET

and the way we manage our
affairs
as if they were dreams
and we
victims
of waking moments
intimidated by visions we choose
but did not want

(where passion destroys us,
hate saves)

in the long nightmare
of our lives
the image of death
looms large
and comforting
like the unconcerned march
of the alarm clock
to the appointed hour

I see the years ahead
marked off in paychecks
(who was it?
in my youth
that circled redly
on each clean calendar
two Fridays a month
leaving this precise incision
on the skin of my brain)

the months behind me stand
like horses left at the starting gate,
dumbly nervous
feigning gestures of helplessness

shadows of time
invite me to insanity
inside the fibrous crystal walls
of broken clocks

"move the hands of your face
and your time will change"
                                        she chimes

cracks in the walls
bleed pendulums, mainsprings
                                and splintered glass
I do not believe her
        but drink her rusty tea
                watching from the corner of my eye
                        waiting for a bell to strike

for Dan Bear

UNFINISHED BUSINESS

"you know how it is
with the old friends you run into
in those damn little cafes
just off the main drag . . ."

five in the morning
again
wondering
how I'd defend this one
to D.
who doesn't care anyway
and already forming lies
for S.
who does

what bothers me
is the lack of emtoion
I feel
contemplating
early sunlight
waking the birds
(even city birds
sing sweetly
but the caged bird
has no voice

will the morning ever come
when this bird
will rise up singing?)

on the street
you will not recognize as yours
the words you created
by laying seige to my body

one thing only
you might call your own;
one morning on your windowsill
a sound of small birds
                                        weeping

for my friend, JB

THE VIEW FROM JB'S WINDOW

looking out on the Bay
the old wharf
and the line of yellow arched piers
that follow the shore a mile up
to G. square and tourist land

distant
this world
from all others
you not only allow
but demand
I be at ease with myself here

we know
the Great Preposterous Duty
my ego has signed my life to,
and the self-indulgent freedom
I envy so much,
are neither more nor less
than other cages

(it is easier to admit these things here,
this stark clarity
a painful incision to the eye)

we become hunger artists
starving on scant visions
obsessed with the absolute

the immensity of our desire
makes gifts unmentionable,
we barter
the shadows that inhabit us

and measure our success
by what we lose

and afterwards
we clothe ourselves in scars
drape our sins around us
as shining armaments
in true Genet style
our betrayals become
our badges of courage

we run in the night
hounding ghosts of names
stalking nightmares
like jungle tribesmen
in the ritual of blood

these passions we thirst for
as if desperate
for some lost innocence,
like the tattooed fingers
searching
for the smooth tissue
beneath the decorated flesh

SONG FOR SUSAN

like a sore
in the skin
I can't get
to the core of
I can't
get it out
from under
my skin
I can't
get it out
from the core
of my skin

core of skin
core of skin . . .

youyou sonofabitch
can't get you outout . . .

the skin peels away
from the kernal
exposing the inner core

this is no extravagance
but strength

get it out
gct it out
core of skin–

peel away
the skin
throw away
the skin

with it go the wounds

what stays
is neither gods nor mans

but yours

Kephra's Disk

my grandfather
worked as a gauger
for humble oil
for thirty five years,
he walked the long fields
from derrick to derrick
adjusting pressure valves
and counting
the big gummy barrelsful
that came
belching out of the earth

he taught his children
how to 'change the wells'
and went bird hunting
for weeks at a time
my mother
tells the story
about the night young bobby
changed the wells
and she and terrell and russell
went tearing down to fix it
before pumps and black gum
went spewing into the air

the day the new foreman
from dallas
tried to fire him
grandpa had been working
in the fields twenty years
he had never
made a mistake in his books
for twenty years
his rolling script
(which wrote love letters
on the side
for the amorous, but illiterate,
young men of Little Rock)
sent in perfect ledgers

but the new foreman
didn't like it
that grandpa had such a perfect record
and so much leisure time, too
so he said
"bledsoe,
the other men
don't like it
that you get paid
for eight hours a day
and spend every afternoon
in the pool hall
with the company car parked outside"
so grandpa told him
any damn fool
could do the job in four
and to prove it,
took him out to the fields
walked the foremans legs off
and did it in three
and the foreman said
"well,
don't leave the company car
in front of the pool hall,
go home and get your own"
but grandpa wouldn't do that either
wasted gas, he said

so the foreman fired him,
grandpa laughed
and went on
to the same fields
he'd worked for twenty years
and nobody dared take over
his route
because you just didn't
mess with
old man bledsoe

when he didn't get his paycheck
in two weeks
he got in the car
and drove to houston
where the district manager
read over the careful report
the foreman had written
calling grandpa 'obstreperous'

the district manager
looked at grandpa's records
he looked at the foreman's report
he looked back at grandpa
who was shouting
"the damn fool fired me!"
and then he transferred the foreman
back to dallas
and told him
"you just can't fire a man like that"

the foreman's wife was mad
the foreman was confused
but grandpa thought he had seen
Justice Administered
and went down to the pool hall
in the company car
to celebrate
and the kids changed the wells

JOHN HENRY

my great grandfather
was the first
presbyterian minister
this side of the mississippi
he wrote a book
about the pope
entitled
"Man of Sin"
and was poisoned
by a catholic priest
they later, of course,
hung the priest
but it didn't do much
for my great grandfather

this event outraged my grandfather
so much
he became a circuit rider
and rode salvation
over most of the continental
United States
and raised his eldest
John Henry
to carry on the line

but in 1917
John Henry
discovered
the Library of Congress
and left home
to become an alcoholic

somewhere
in the depression years
of the mid-30's
he was in a boom town
in Oklahoma

working as a geologist
and practicing his real profession
on saturday nights
when he and the bunkhouse boys
went to a stomp dance
and got drunk on Kiamish Mountain moonshine
and stayed up all night
discussing
the deeper side of life,
at dawn
John Henry found himself
in front of the bathroom mirror
straightening his tie
and spit polishing his
8½ EEEEE Florsheim Wingtips

that was the last he remembered
when he woke up
monday afternoon

during the following week
he observed a certain
diffidence with which
people treated him
but, being a snob anyway
he accepted it
as his rightful due
and thought
nothing of it
till thursday
when the town preacher
stopped him in the street
saying
"John, you should go back
to the faith of your fathers.
That sermon you gave
Sunday
was the most inspiring
I've ever heard."

John Henry thanked him
graciously,
asked about
Mabel and the kids,
made a quick exit
around the corner
to a friend he could trust
and asked
"What the *hell*
did I do Sunday?"
his friend thought
that was the funniest thing
he'd heard in years
"You mean, you don't remember?
Why, you got religion
and preached hell,
fire and brimstone
and led everybody down
to the river
for baptism."

John pondered
on the fact
that such a thing
could drive a man
to give up drink
whereupon
his friend replied
"But John,
look at it this way;
you saved
thirty souls."

that was when
my father said
he gave up god

WILLARD

it would be hard to say
if I was a friend
to Willard or not
I had seen him
that evening
given him a short hug
and thought
he was looking better
then I'd ever seen him

that night
September 6, 1974
Willard Cummings Moser
shot himself twice
in the head
with a .45

I inherited
his hand massager
a Random House Dictionary
and his 16 year old son

Willard's mother
took care of the funeral
six of us
sat on the back row
enduring his mother's friends
who hadn't seen Willard
since he was twelve
as they sat around
giggling about whosit's baby
and *poor Mrs. Moser*
"You know why it's a closed casket
don't you? They say . . ."

and I wanted to get up and shout
"NONE OF YOU EVER KNEW WILLARD!
ALL YOU BITCHES GET OUT!
OUT!"

but I restrained myself
up to the first time
the preacher said
Willard
then I ate six kleenex immediately
so poor Chris
had to drive the car
20 miles an hour
through a steel Texas drizzle
from Port Arthur
to the cemetery in Beaumont
where Willard knew
who his friends were,
Chris and J. Roger and I
slooshed through the mud
to give Steve jr.
a valium
which I dropped
in front of the preacher
Robert retrieved it quick
popped it into Steve's mouth
and none of the family said
anything

but it wasn't until Steve
started pulling the casket bouquet
apart,
red carnations
Willard's favorite,
handing them out individually
like small red faces
that Chris fell apart

he told me
he wanted to have
his carnation pressed and saved
I said
as far as I was concerned
nothing doing
we weren't gonna
FORGET
Willard, anyway
he said I was right

Chris went home
with Elroy and Al
and Roger and I went home
with the family
for cake and coffee
and later that night
brought the child home
to Houston
where he belonged

a few days later
standing in my kitchen
washing the dishes
that had accumulated
my grandmother
walked in
and began to tell me
about the time
in the oil fields
one of the men
got his arm caught
in the rig belt
and it stretched
14 feet
before they got him loose
and all the time
him beggin for mercy
beggin for someone

to kill him
but he died
soon enough anyway

she went on to say
his whole family
all seven kids and wife
had been moved
into her and grandpa's tent
and cookin and fixin
and cleanin and messin
for people
when someone was dead
was sure a lot of trouble
but it was
just
one of those things
you had
to put up with

she should have known
she had been dead
20 years

THERE IS STILL SOMETHING TO BE SAID FOR STATE PRIDE
—or—
THIS DOESN'T NEED A TITLE BECAUSE EVERYBODY KNOWS IT ANYWAY

got into the City wed. night
                    3 am
spent the next morning
appeasing my brother
for my rude timing
tracking down
my first cappuccino
       55¢ at Cafe Trieste on Grant St.
              had gone up a dime
                     since last there
another wall of home photographs
added
one layer of graffiti
painted over
            and begun again
otherwise
all the same
young Giani (pronounced Johnny)
working two handles
                 one milk nozzle
same fat faced
middle aging waitress
stuffing pastries
down her face
and barking at customers

sat down by Laurence
the Mayor of North Beach
he remembered
everything about me
                 but my name

asked at the Coffee Gallery
and got an address
only six digits off
found John the Bartender
and lost my leather carrying case
                    for papers
helping to turn
the first stone
of the City

went home
knowing
I'd put it off long enough
dialed the phone
for a disgruntled David
surprise
apprehension
I'll meet you in front of
                    Western Union
in an hour

down to pick up the cabled money
from my old man
in Houston
thinking
David has an old lady
I have an old man
minus one and minus one
make a negative two

D. is late
I finish my business
before walking out
                    on Market St. again
choking on too many words
not enough courage to say
                    any of them
look both ways
the street is deserted this late
                    in the evening

30 yards away
tall and thinner than I remember
hair so close cropped
it seems
almost non-existent
blue jeans
blue jean jacket
blue shirt
I do not recognize him
but I know it is
I give myself
a few seconds to run
or scream or faint
but the magnet
is already working
I turn back around
lie
"You're right, I didn't recognize you."
wondering
will all our lines be lies

we go to Spec's
where props and scenes
never change
only the script is revised
each season
D. is leary of the Beach
afraid, but silent
                    in his fears
to be seen with me
but I still want to see
Vesuvio's TV room
overlooking Columbus and Broadway
where we find Wayne
encouraging a new battle scar
won from
falling down Vesuvio's stairs
dead drunk
one Saturday night

I am not impressed
but Wayne
is as pretty as ever
I pat his hand
thinking
what a delightful toy
you would make
for some rich bitch
                                        back home
I should ask the price
before I leave
the commodities market there
could use new blood

David and I
trudge beer glasses
upstairs, Wayne to join us
discussing
coffee houses, Houston,
the characters left
raving the streets in
                              North Beach
and why Whitebird
is remembered
but not mentioned

it is a good hour
before Wayne leaves
David
insists we move closer
to the window
closer to each other
his hands and kisses
take my face
and he says
he loves me

I think quietly
"you will not say
                                        such things
later on tonight"
and I am right
enough booze
and bullshit
down to business now
"come up to my place
for a while,
Nibs is out of town"

bum a pipeful
from Wayne and Monique downstairs
D. reading Bukowski to me
cats and poems
tumbled on the carpet
into the bedroom
doffing lights and clothes quickly
hesitation is for liars

force
cruelty
pleasure
spinning
on the fortune wheel
the sphinx-faced operator
suddenly smiles at me
through nameless wooden horses
one word
steampipes to my brain
                                        "I didn't know how much I
needed . . ."
I have no choice
but to be content
with this half confession

next day
a phone call
to the effect
Monique
has had a long talk
with Nibs
and all hell has broken loose
–don't call me
I'll call you

I travel into the City
buy a carnation for my lapel
sip my cappuccino
last time I was here
it took me a good two weeks
to ruin David's love life
this time
less than 48 hours

next time
perhaps they'll learn
to take Texans
more seriously

Voice

LESSON

"always begin a poem
with the last line"
                              he said
so naturally it was three years
before I knew
he was a backasswards cancer
like myself

used to think of it
as a brand,
now they call it Style

as all handicaps
it has its advantages,
between the vision
and the form
a complex play of blind will
and reverse time

write the script
and not see it for years,
but thats cheap
some never do

the strength of will
to kill yourself
dictates the number of others
you require to love you,
you are beautiful
proportionate to the pain inside

a rational discovery
nudges you in the ribs
at a dinner party with yourself
". . . hey,
she wants to kill you . . ."
a civilized ego
measures the game
lives off the ante
of the house demons

if a poem is worth
8 months, 5 fingernails
a beer over the head
and a left to the jaw
in a bar brawl,
you still can't buy lunch
with it
but it might get you laid

which is to say
the difference between self-indulgence
and honesty
is purely hypothetical/arbitrary
not to mention
subjective

life as a discipline/tool
is an exercise in repetition/reflection
the spiral upward/completion
is the decision
and the destiny
we have the right
and the responsibility
to become
what we love and fear most

religion defines it as fate
the scientist calls it the "leap of faith"
a gambler trusts his poker face

call it anything
don't quibble the price
begin a poem
with the last line

alabaster face looking out
some dark window
of the soul

whose lover are you
that approaches
from my moon-blind side?

I hear your animal boast
your mother
invoked the stars
and the sun
was secretly your father

your human whispers
that love
can make a difference
in our lives
if we let it

and the spirit
stirs the blood
to murmur
"Alabaster,
face me fully
and the shrunken scars
of your womb
will be filled with light
and night travelers
will once again
know your face."

FOR HOWARD

love
not being
romance,
or even
the romance of martyrdom,
it was Nan
who said
"we need a new mythology,
one that doesn't romanticize
pain"
after telling me
she wanted to follow Dove
to New Mexico
and shoot him in the leg
for leaving her
with a note on the kitchen table
that said
he was going
down to the store for milk

and
not being
eros,
at midnight thirty
hank calls me
to say sorry he hasn't written
but he was presently
being inundated
by one
Cupcakes O'Brian
and I said
"hank,
I think I understand,
really. . . ."

and
not being
what my father died of,
a drunk leaving
a sick wife
two kids with polio
and a later-to-be-poet
neurotic
with no money and no insurance

not being
any of these things–
(let me say this;
I did not know
what gentleness meant
before you came)
rather
something
that imparts strength
not seasonal
but constant
and above all
something
that does not demand change
but seeks
and works
this wonder
through its own subtlety

love
being these things
and your face
then let them come
to strike upon the door
and cry out the question,

I will not deny you
though the cock strike dawn
and they ask three times
I will answer
with the truth of your face

and it will be said
I am an honest woman

RECIPE

morning

the sun sifts through these curtains
a white stream
of flour

I stand at the window
the light settling on me
this pose always reminds me
of you

who binds my life
like the rich, sulfur yellow yolks

I take my sweetness
from the deep brown of memories

milk the air for words

take hope
to raise my heart

in the window
I turn honey gold
with the morning light

I am
my own
daily bread

24

I'm 24
having my third book published
and still
it's wrong
I take half a mandrex
don't feel it at all
and realize I'm getting slightly
strung out
again,
my doctor won't prescribe
this kind of medicine
says I don't need it,
he doesn't know me well
medical school told him
I need a lot of appointments
at $35 a hit

my knees buckle
going out to see
who's breaking beer bottles
on the sidewalk
and I think
maybe it's not as bad
as I thought
with the downers,
it's just the depression
I can't see through

in two weeks
I go into the schools
to teach kids
how to "write poetry"
as if I knew
my mother is proud of me
her daughter, the poet

everybody loves or hates
but knows me as
"the poet"
and my mind snaps back
to the cruel, quick note
handed me in North Beach
where, at the age of 20,
I was reading for free beer
in the Coffee Gallery
the note said
"you are *not* a poet
because
you fuck
too many men"
I loved the man
who wrote the note
and fucked the others
because he didn't love me

later that night
he wanted me to go home with him
to his bathroomless hotel room
and fuck all screaming night
but not tell
his old lady
in the morning
and I went home
with his best friend

now
I'm 24
and learning
David was right
when he said
"you've got to live with yourself
and *take it*"

tuna fish
most of the time
hamburger and porkchops
just after pay day
I can see
Leonardo Da Vinci's mother saying
"What *else* can I do
with pasta?"

the dream is;
maybe next year
I'll have some money together
and, if I can con
a bank
into fronting me a loan
to buy a house,
I'll have a
permanent depression point
which is a lot
for someone
who grew up
like I did
not to say
I didn't have a home
Oh sure
I had one of those
a two bedroom house
for four people
on Belcrest
where my brother almost broke my back
one night
for letting one of our 22 guinea pigs
get loose in the bushes
later
one of them
got mouse fever

and Hazel had them all
put to sleep
while we were at school
we had to have shots
and went around
depressed for weeks
we knew
she never really liked
the damn things anyway

when I was twelve
Bill and Eric
were gone
and Hazel needed a hysterectomy
or went nuts
they gave her an operation
and six months of shock treatments
(I was never sure
which came first)
I lived with my aunt in Chicago
who beat up her husband
with pewter candlesticks,
the colored maid and I
would hide in the attic
while she screamed
"Die, damn you!
Why don't you just have a heart attack
and die?!"
and Uncle Phil said kindly
"Now Irene . . ."
while she broke
his glasses
and I contemplated
throwing myself down the stairs
to get their minds off the fight,

afterwards
I would go down
and cover up the scratches
on Phil's face
with her make-up,
listen to him lie
to his optometrist
(who had heard it before)
about how
all three pairs of his glasses
had "accidentally'
gotten broken
and watch him drive off
praying he would make it
downtown
because he couldn't see shit
without them

then I would go feed Irene
vienna sausages and crackers
while she told me
how mean he was to her

when I got back
Hazel was still
in the hospital
and had a little card by her bed
with her name
and the date
written on it,
she would finger it
with a bewildered look
as if she knew
it meant something important
but couldn't remember
exactly what

and I stayed
with the family of the janitor
of the Mormon Church
whose 16 year old daughter
had just married an ex-con
and sat around the house
in her night gown
telling me
how much she regretted
having sex with her husband
two days
before they were married,

and the father would take me off
in a corner of the church
and plant big slimy
tobacco and beer-stained kisses
on my lips
telling me about
"Brotherly Love"

then I stayed
with a nice lutheran family
whose old man
smoked a pipe
and never
had any inclination to make a pass
at me
even though his wife
had a thyroid problem
and was going bald

Hazel got out of the hospital
right after that
I went home
and learned to take care of her

two years later
she came out of her stupor
and realized
I made the decisions for myself
as well as for her
and did as I damn well pleased
so she gave away
my german shepherd
and beat hell out of me
till I left
on her birthday
two years later

and Hannah wants to know
if I'll go to the Caribbean next year
to get the restlessness
out of my blood,
not knowing
itchy feet is something
I can handle
it's the other things,
like insanity,
that are rough

the old crap
spills out of my head
in long movie reels,
I stuff it back in
and go talk
to millionaires' wives
in their big houses,
agree with them
about the hard lives they've had
because I need their money
for my poetry projects
and think about
Fitzgerald's bone,

wondering
how much of it I gnaw
how much
is stuck in my throat

words
arrive in my hands
already wearing coffins
I stack them all
on top of my head
till I carry so much weight
I stand out in a crowd
like someone
balancing a boulder

people say
I have
"influence"